BIG BEND LANDSCAPES

NUMBER TWELVE

Joe and Betty Moore Texas Art Series

BIG BEND LANDSCAPES

Dennis Blagg

INTRODUCTION BY RON TYLER

Texas A&M University Press
College Station

Thunderhead, 2001

The paper used in this book meets the minimum require-
ments of the American National Standard for Permanence
of Paper for Printed Library Materials, z39.48-1984.
Binding materials have been chosen for durability.

*The generous support of Harris, Finley & Bogle, P.C., of Fort
Worth, Texas, helped make the publication of this book possible.*

LIBRARY OF CONGRESS
CATALOGING-IN-PUBLICATION DATA

Blagg, Dennis, 1951–
Big Bend landscapes / Dennis Blagg ;
introduction by Ron Tyler. — 1st ed.
p. cm. — (Joe and Betty Moore Texas art series ; no. 12)
Includes bibliographical references.
ISBN 1–58544–202–X
1. Blagg, Dennis, 1951— Catalogs.   2. Big Bend
Region (Tex.)—In art—Catalogs.
I. Title.   II. Series.
ND237.B5965 A4   2002
759.13–DC21   2002001548

CONTENTS

Sleeping Lion
1997
Oil on Canvas
5" × 15"
The Frank H. Wardlaw Collection of Texas Art
Texas A&M University Press

I see a sleeping lion in this rock formation. I've caught it as a dead haze has set in, so it is barely visible. The pollution problem is getting worse as the years pass. I hope that something can be done soon, because a national park that is un-matched in its diversity and beauty is at stake. Time is running out, and all of us should be concerned. The Big Bend National Park will be the lost treasure of our National Park System.

ARTIST'S PREFACE

LANDSCAPE PAINTING in America has endured the test of time. Like Haley's Comet, the movement of landscape painting keeps coming back again and again. The importance of depicting nature in painting owes its roots to European art, which no doubt started with the large-scale portrait painting, with grand views of nature as its background. With the growth of the Hudson River School in North America the mantle of landscape painting fell into the capable hands of such artists as Thomas Cole and Frederick Church, among others. A more western view developed with artists Thomas Moran and Albert Bierstadt's depictions of the Grand Canyon, Yellowstone, and other westerly wonders. Many of these artists were driven by a great sense of mission in their work—the purity of nature as something divine. Many of these artists shared the same environmental concerns about the conquest of the American landscape.

Today's artists are no different, though their concerns about keeping in step with a more modernist outlook seem to dominate their vision. Art always has more selfish reasons for moving forward—it seeks to challenge our perceptions and attitudes of the world around us. Today's landscape painters seek to expand the horizon of what they see as the formalities of painting. Like other modern artists, they are concerned with the very same issues that all painting presents: compositional integrity, linear design, color, as well as the surface tension of raw paint. These issues seem to go beyond their mission to save nature; they feed their desire to make art. Artists such as Neil Welliver, Harold Gregor, Forest Moses, and other contemporaries have always had the same goal: to make great art.

I have been deeply influenced by this movement of landscape painting, as well as by abstract painting. I first encountered art when, at age eight, I opened my mother's large books of works by Michelangelo and Leonardo da Vinci. We lived on a cotton farm near Lubbock in western Texas. I was captured by the magic of the paintings. I am a twin, the fifth child of a family of ten children. Growing up, we were always outside, hunting rattlesnakes and engaging in many other dangerous adventures.

After my father's failed attempt to lure our attention with rubber snakes, my mother brought home some paper and crayons for us. We would draw for hours—rattlesnakes, hawks, cowboys and Indians. We would also draw from many of the pictures in those two heavy books that my mother treasured, with strict instructions not to damage anything.

Moving from West Texas was a most difficult time for all of us. Leaving the country and moving to the city seemed so wrong. At least that is what our dog, Skipper, thought; he ran away after only a couple of days of living in Dallas. I grew up working at the truck stop that my father and mother ran and had my share of near-death experiences there. The war in Vietnam called, so I was rescued by military service, serving an interesting tour in South Korea as a U.S. Army illustrator. After my experience as an illustrator, I knew that commercial art was not for me. I remember my first trip to the Dallas Museum of Art as being an eye-opener for me. What I remember most was how certain paintings held such a life of their own—they were not static.

My only experience in seeing art had been limited to books until my fateful trip to the museum revealed how much energy a real painting can hold. Innes, Hopper, Henri, Eakins, Church, and Moran were all there. I had at last found what I was seeking. For me they represented all that I wanted to be—a painter.

I have always felt a great sense of humility in painting the landscape of the Big Bend National Park. There is a stark, sobering reality to what lies before me that cannot be put into words. For more than twenty years I have loaded up the Jeep and traveled to that jagged and monolith-filled landscape. I journey there for two reasons: one, to find my center and get my bearings; and two, to take as many photos as I can, which I use as sources for my paintings. My use of photographs is largely as a base to build from, not a means to an end. I shoot so many pictures of one location that the result is a convincing collage of the landscape I am painting. This is like creating my own reality, moving things around to meet my expectations.

Many people have commented on the light in my paintings as portraying their own experience in being in Big Bend and seeing the landscape themselves. I believe that others notice this because my sense of color is so ingrained in that landscape. My colors are not based on the photograph; they are based on my feeling from being there. More than anything, it is "being" there that matters the most. For me this sense of being there is what the experience is all about. The photographic images I take back to my studio in Fort Worth play such a small part in what I am trying to do. When I begin a painting I go there again, subconsciously. In a way I am there all the time. The Big Bend has become such a part of me that some say I have internalized it.

The paintings and drawings in this book span some twenty years, a long time. I have come to know the Big Bend so well that I do not merely paint its landscape. Instead, it is as if I paint a portrait of a place. For me the Big Bend has become a landscape full of symbolism. The cacti, rocks, and sky provide sanctuary as well as inspiration. These paintings are about the duality of the literal and mythical, an exploration that goes beyond the real. The desert represents a landscape of broken promise, yet it is a place of vast spiritual content—an emptiness waiting to be fulfilled. The desert is also a place in constant transition, an ever-changing reality. From the coolness of early dawn to the stagnant heat of midday to the spiritual finality of sunset, the Big Bend offers me many faces to paint.

ACKNOWLEDGMENTS

I HAVE MANY PEOPLE to thank for many different reasons. First, thanks to Diane for her support and encouragement throughout our life together. Thanks to my mother for keeping those two wonderful books—of the work of Leonardo da Vinci and Michelangelo—within the reach of a child's hand. I appreciate the assistance of Daniel Blagg, my twin brother. He understands how difficult it is to be a painter. My thanks to Mi Mi Kilgore who has been like a guardian angel throughout my life. I owe her so much. Special thanks go to Bill Otton, Louise Chapman, and all the wonderful people at the Museum of South Texas in Corpus Christi. To those who have traveled to the Big Bend National Park with

me—Vernon Fisher, Jim Malone, and Harry Rosenthal—thanks for your patience when I needed to stop to record a moment.

Many people helped put together this book. I greatly appreciate Ron Tyler's contribution. Many thanks go to Emilie Butz for her many hours of work during the early part of this endeavor. I also would like to thank Leslie Lanzotti and Betty Alcorn for pitching in from time to time. Special thanks to Linda Beaupré who helped guide me through this difficult process, and many thanks go to Annette Coolidge, who shot the transparencies of all my pencil drawings, and to Billy Stone, for his photographs of "Fresno One" and "Late Drive."

The photograph of "Dry Ocotillos" is courtesy of the San Antonio Museum of Art. "Nugent Mountain" is courtesy of the Museum of Fine Arts, Houston. The remaining forty-six photographs are my own.

Thanks to Charlie Harris, Dee Finley, and everyone associated with the law firm of Harris, Finley & Bogle, P. C., of Fort Worth, Texas, for their contribution to this project. I appreciate those at Texas A&M University Press for their hard work and encouragement in publishing this book. Finally, I want to thank Meredith Long and all the wonderful folks at Meredith Long Gallery for supporting me and helping make this book possible.

BIG BEND LANDSCAPES

THE BIG BEND COUNTRY

Ron Tyler

Another branch of these mountains diverges about the head of the Pecos, and running south with unequal elevation, crosses the Rio Bravo. . . , forming the great bend in that river, and producing one of the most remarkable features on the face of the globe—that of a river traversing at an oblique angle a chain of lofty mountains, and making through these, on a gigantic scale, what is called in Spanish America a cañon—that is, a river hemmed in by vertical walls.

William H. Emory
Report on the United States and Mexican Boundary Survey, 1857

THE BIG BEND COUNTRY comes upon you by surprise. No matter which direction you come from, you will have traversed hundreds of miles of flat, dusty prairie, gone through scrubby little towns that could have provided the Hollywood stereotype for "Last Chance Gulch" if they didn't, and marveled at the stamina of anyone who would try to eke out a living on such a God-forsaken patch if they didn't own an oil well.

The first signs of a change are the mountains. They begin as timid little mounds on the far-distant horizon, but as you approach them they gradually reveal their true identities as genuine if not quite Rocky-Mountain-grade promontories.

Continuing down the road, mesas, canyons, and draws complicate this terrain, which the Spaniards called the *despoblado*—the uninhabited, and uninhabitable, land—until, finally, a scenic and jagged and apparently lost clump of the Rockies, the Chisos Mountains, appears. This isolated mountain group, a timbered and temperate island in a sea of sand and rock, marks the heart of the Big Bend Country of Texas. It is home to dozens of alpine flora and fauna, some found only here, that are marooned on its peaks. This is a special place, set apart for centuries by its isolation and ruggedness, and made accessible only by the ease of twentieth-century travel. The Big Bend is one of the remotest and most subtly beautiful do-

mains in the entire U.S. National Park System.

The park itself, established in 1944, comprises more than 800,000 acres nestled in the crook of the Rio Grande and stretches more than 100 miles along the Texas-Chihuahua-Coahuila border southeast of El Paso in Brewster County. It is flanked on the northeast by the 105,708-acre Black Gap Wildlife Management Area and on the west by the recently acquired 279,640-acre Big Bend Ranch State Park, both owned by the State of Texas.

The larger Big Bend Country encompasses a substantial chunk of territory bounded by the Rio Grande on the south and an imaginary arc from, roughly, the Rio Grande villages of Candelaria and Ruidoso on the west, northeastward some fifty miles to Marfa, then, paralleling the Southern Pacific Railroad tracks eastward for more than 100 miles, to the cities of Alpine, Marathon, and Sanderson. South of the river is the even more remote Bolsón de Mapimí, part of the larger Chihuahuan Desert, which also embraces the Sierra de Santa Elena, Sierra de San Vicente, and Sierra del Carmen in the northern Mexican states of Chihuahua and Coahuila. The Big Bend has always been an out-of-the-way place, visited only by the adventurous, the patient, or the lost.

The story that comes closest to explaining the region's origins, based at least on the looks of the place, is the Indian legend of the Great Creator who threw all his trash into a huge pile in a remote part of West Texas after he had finished his creating. From a distance, one might imagine how the Comanches and Apaches, who rode back and forth across the region throughout the year, viewed this godly rubble. Perhaps these peaks were a refuge from the desert's blinding heat, or a source of strong medicine for the People, who sought their spirits in high places. The story lives on because it gets at the scarred, disheveled, inhospitable, and seemingly random nature of this portion of the earth's face, which in the Big Bend ranges from 7,000-foot-high mountains to 1,500-foot-deep canyons and everything in between.

This exotic expanse of desert and mountain, a popular conception of nature in its "original chaotic state," enjoys new prominence in these days of desert chic, when miles of sandy, prickly-pear studded, and rock-strewn badlands conjure up visions of dude ranch vacations and spectacular evening sunsets instead of the more primordial concerns of survival. As J. Frank Dobie once remarked, "The greatest happiness possible to a man. . . is to become civilized, to know the pageant of the past, to love the beautiful. . . and then, retaining his animal instincts and appetites, to live in a wilderness."[1] The Big Bend annually casts its wilderness spell over the thousands who visit the national park, whether bikers and river runners from Austin, developers from Houston, or cowboys from a nearby ranch; but it is more than that for some like Fort Worth artist Dennis Blagg, who like the Comanche and the Apache of a previous century, returns year after year. An artist since childhood, Blagg was primarily a figure and cityscape painter when he saw the Big Bend. Then, as he says, he "just stopped painting figures and began to paint landscape." For him the Big Bend continues to be a source of strong medicine. It "is a landscape full of symbolism," Blagg says, "a place of vast spiritual content. . . a mystical spirituality" that speaks to his "inner core."[2]

Perhaps the strength that Blagg feels here is similar to that derived for centuries by the Pueblo-like Indians the Spaniards called Jumanos. They probably migrated down the Rio Grande from higher and more civilized altitudes in what is today New Mexico to the junction of the Río Conchos and Rio Grande, sometime between 1200 and 1400. The Spaniards called at least two groups Jumanos: the Puebloan culture at La Junta, and a tribe of nomadic hunters in the Chisos and Davis Mountains. Early historians haven't paid much attention to them, but their extensive remnants—baskets, pottery, and tools collected by early-twentieth-century Harvard archeologists, and metates, smoke-blackened rocky cliffs, and pictographs that survive in many of the canyons and caves along the river—tell of their meager existence. The Rio Grande supplied the basic elements of their life, but it was an unreliable sustainer, flooding at times and dwindling to a mere rivulet at others.[3]

By the time Cabeza de Vaca visited these "People of the Cows" around 1535, he found them in such desperate condition that they were eating their seeds instead of planting them. Perhaps because of a severe drought, they had dispersed to a friendlier and more reliable climate—the tributaries of the Pecos and Colorado Rivers—by the time Franciscan friar Agustín Rodríguez visited the area in 1581. The Jumanos again brought themselves to the attention of the Spaniards a century later when, in October, 1683, Chief Juan Sabeata petitioned for missionary and military assistance. They seem to disappear from the historical record after 1700, but some scholars think that the survivors might have evolved into the tribe that we know as the Kiowas.

For the next century and one-half, the *despoblado* served Mescalero and Lipan Apaches and Comanches less as a sanctuary and more as a natural sieve that filtered out pursuing enemies. These tribes made much of their living by raiding fringe settlements on both the Anglo and Mexican frontiers, then retreating into Comanchería via the Great Comanche Trail. The trail began in their South Plains stronghold, along what is today the Texas–New Mexico boundary, and extended southeastward in two forks, crossing some of the most desolate regions of the Llano Estacado. The northern fork probably followed part of Coronado's 1541 route through Blanco Canyon, while the southern route followed various creeks and draws to the northern fork of the Double Mountain Fork of the Brazos River, then turned southward through Yellow House Canyon, southeast of Lubbock. Once off the plains, the two trails merged north of present-day Big Spring, sweeping in a southwesterly direction to cross the Pecos at Horsehead Crossing. Continuing southwestward, the trail passed the vicinity of present-day Fort Stockton and Marathon, then turned southward into the Big Bend and again split. The main route crossed the Rio Grande near Chisos Ford, between Santa Elena and Mariscal Canyons. It also branched off to cross near the Hot Springs on the Rio Grande, between Mariscal and Boquillas Canyons. The other fork crossed near present-day Lajitas. Colonel Emilio Langberg, military inspector of the Chihuahua frontier, described the trail as being "wider than any 'royal road'" and "so well beaten that it appears that suitable engineers had constructed it."[4]

There are well-known place names and landmarks throughout the region—usually mesas, hills, mountains, or springs—where the Apaches and Comanches lived and often went to get their medicine. The quest for medicine was one of the most important rituals that young men undertook. At puberty, a boy would cleanse himself and seclude himself from the camp—on a nearby hill, near a tree, or, perhaps, in a "vision pit."[5] There he fasted for four days, or until he received a vision, which would be the source of his power throughout his life. Hills also served as landmarks and observation points.[6] The Plains Indians had a strong interest in and sense of the land, and this intimacy is acknowledged in place names, some of which still exist. The Medicine Mounds in Hardeman County might be the best known of these sites, but extant place names document the Indian presence in the Big Bend as well. The Chisos Mountains, probably named for a group of Chizo Indians who lived there, might be the best example. The Mexicans knew Kokernot Springs, near present-day Alpine, as *el Charco de Alsate,* the waterhole of Alsate, the famous Apache chief who lived in the Big Bend. Alsate's name, which may, in fact, be a corruption of the Spanish name Arzate, also appears on Alsate Creek, Alsate's Face in Green Gulch in Big Bend National Park, and *Cueva de Alsate,* Alsate's Cave, in the Chisos Mountains.[7] A legend of old Indian fighters who lived along the Rio Grande claims that the Santiago Range, south of present-day Marathon, was named for Don Santiago, a Chisos chief.[8] And Comanche Springs, in the southeastern part of what is today Fort Stockton in central Pecos County, was one of the main watering holes along the Comanche trail.[9]

Captain José de Berroterán, commander of the Mexican presidios of Mapimí and Concho, seems representative of the Spanish frustration in dealing with these Indians. Having once again failed to catch some Apaches after a 1729 raid, he complained that this "gulf or pocket [of land] . . . contains steep places, dry places, few waterholes, and great distances. . . . For this reason it cannot be inhabited nor populated by rational Christians." Governor Juan de Ugalde had a little more success half a century later. With campaigns over a decade, he was able in 1789 to conclude treaties with several of the most troublesome tribes and disperse others throughout the region. By the turn of the nineteenth century, Spanish knowledge of the region had grown to the point that their maps included several villages, the Chisos Mountains, and even the point—probably near Lipan Crossing—where Ugalde crossed the river.[10] But Ugalde knew that he had only bought a little time in this frontier clash. The *despoblado* remained a part of Comanchería until the Anglo Americans arrived.

The Indians must have known that their time in the Trans-Pecos was drawing to a close by the 1830s, when commercial caravans began to pass through the country headed for Chihuahua. Their number had increased by the late 1840s, as literally dozens of parties crossed the Trans-Pecos each year. The immediate catalysts were the Mexican War and U.S. annexation of the Southwest, the 1848 discovery of gold in California, and the subsequent horde of immigrants who brought that state into the Union in 1850. Some gold seekers, in their rush to get to California, cut from Austin or San Antonio across the Trans-Pecos rather than take one of the longer but safer routes across Panama or around the Horn.[11] C. C. Cox of Harrisburg, who crossed the area with a group headed for California in June, 1849, found that "An occasional Rattle Snake was the only living creature to be seen, But the bones of many a noble horse lay whitening upon the Earth, relics of the savage feast, or victims of the warriors speed. . . ."[12] By the 1850s, surveying parties crisscrossed the Big Bend Country, and railroad construction crews arrived after the Civil War.

Strange as it may seem, many of the newly arriving Anglo Americans also drew spiritual nourishment from this barren place. These newcomers were the intellectual children of European romanticism, the revolutionary philosophical movement that originated in eighteenth-century Germany and swept through France and England on its way to America. Reacting against the rigid hierarchies of neoclassicism, proponents of romanticism empowered the individual with ultimate authority, rather than, for example, the church or the state. "The eighteenth century had been an age of classification," wrote historian Hugh Honor. "Insects, plants, animals and the races of man were divided into genera, species and sub species." The intent was to discover the Divine Order of nature, but instead such scrutiny merely documented its many differences. The mid-nineteenth-century romantics then called on the individual to resolve what the corporate community could not. "Trust your own genius," wrote American artist Washington Allston, "listen to the voice within you, and sooner or later she will make herself understood not only to you, but she will enable you to translate her language to the world."[13]

Many Americans, it seems, found their "voice within" in the wilderness. Lacking Europe's documented history with its medieval ruins, American writers and philosophers like Philip Freneau and Estwick Evans in the early 1800s turned to America's ancient wildernesses for examples of the aesthetic concepts of the picturesque and the sublime. At the same time, deism suggested that the virgin wilderness was the untarnished handiwork of the Creator. Rather than the "hideous and desolate wilderness" of their ancestors, or even the pragmatic commercialism of many of their contemporaries, who understood wilderness only in terms of real estate or timber, emerging American romantics looked to untrammeled nature itself as the defining characteristic of the new nation.[14]

Of course, the Indians could have told them that there was no virgin wilderness in America, that they had hunted in, lived in, farmed, burned, and otherwise shaped it for centuries. But such factual niceties had no place in nineteenth-century American thought.

This romantic view of the American wilderness led the young Thomas Cole in 1823 to turn from portrait painting to depicting "the wild and great features of nature: mountainous forests that know not man."[15] "In civilized Europe the primitive features of scenery have long since been destroyed or modified," he explained in 1835, but "American scenery. . . has features, and glorious ones, unknown to Europe," and its "most distinctive, and perhaps the most impressive, characteristic. . . is its wildness."[16] In canvas after canvas of the Hudson River valley and New England forests, Cole offered morality lessons through his wilderness constructions.

At the same time, the growing transcendentalist religious movement drew God and nature even closer together. "Man cannot afford to be a naturalist to look at Nature directly," wrote Henry David Thoreau, one of the movement's leading proponents. "He must look through and beyond her."[17] Charles W. Webber, author, critic, and editor of the *American Review* under the pseudonym Charles Winterfield, amplified Thoreau's meaning when he wrote of ornithologist and artist John James Audubon's work that it led "through nature up to nature's God."[18] In other words, American romantics, like the

Comanches and Apaches, went into the wilderness to listen for their "inner voice." Landscape artist Worthington Whittredge illustrated the point in telling of a conversation he had with the famous Kit Carson, mountain man, scout, soldier, and Indian agent, during his 1865–66 trip across the plains to Colorado and New Mexico. After watching Whittredge sketch, the diffident Carson described to him a "sunrise he had once seen high up in the Sangre de Cristo. He told how the sun rose behind their dark tops and how it began little by little to gild the snow on their heads, and finally how the full blaze of light came upon them, and the mists began to rise from out the deep canyons, and he wanted to know if I couldn't paint it for him. Nature had made a deep impression on this man's mind, and I could not but think of him standing alone on the top of a great mountain far away from all human contact, worshiping in his way a grand effect of nature until it entered into his soul and made him a silent but thoughtful human being."[19]

That combination of wilderness as representative of America and source of its spiritual essence led to fledgling efforts to preserve various parts of the wilderness, or at least lament their passing as civilization threatened them. It also led to the enormous popularity of landscape painting throughout much of the nineteenth century. Americans wanted to experience their native wilderness—the Hudson River valley, the forests of New England, the Rocky Mountains, Yellowstone, Yosemite, and the Grand Canyon—and

Frederic Church, Albert Bierstadt, Thomas Moran, and dozens of other landscape artists answered the call.

Americans understood. George Hughes, in his book celebrating the fiftieth anniversary of the Methodist Tuesday Meetings for the Promotion of Holiness, related the testimony of Mrs. Mary D. James, who recalled "a visit to a picture gallery, where she saw. . . one of Bierstadt's lovely paintings—a landscape of rare beauty. On one side was a black cloud, which looked tremendous; on the other side the sun shone luminously, the cloud not intercepting its rays as the light fell on the beautiful green hills and the winding river, and the sunlight seemed more beautiful because of the cloud. The tempest and cloud of trial to God's people only reveal more clearly the glory of grace and salvation. We would not know half of the glory of this wonderful salvation were it not for the cloud and the tempest. She thanked God from the depth of her soul for trials which revealed more gloriously the light of God's countenance."[20]

This was the mindset of the first scientific expedition to explore and document the Big Bend in the 1850s. It came during the era of great western reconnaissances, in the tradition of Captain John Charles Frémont of the Topographical Engineers, who had opened up the Far West to the public through his books and maps, after the war with Mexico and simultaneously with the exploration of the newly acquired Southwestern territories, and just as Congress

was authorizing the great Pacific Railroad Survey. Two different private expeditions had failed to open up a wagon road from San Antonio and Austin through the Trans-Pecos to El Paso in 1848 and 1849. In 1850 Colonel John James Abert, commander of the Topographical Engineers, believing that the best road lay along the thirty-second parallel and that nothing less than the "integrity of the Union" was at stake, assigned Brevet Lieutenant Colonel Joseph E. Johnston, a hero of the recent war with Mexico and chief topographical engineer for Texas, to improve upon their work. "Unless some easy, cheap, and rapid means of communicating with these distant provinces be accomplished," Abert predicted, "there is danger, great danger, that they will not constitute parts of our Union."[21]

A Virginian who had graduated from West Point and served in the Seminole war before heading to Mexico, Johnston instructed his engineers to survey the known roads—those charted by John C. Hays and Captain Samuel Highsmith of the Texas Rangers and Robert S. Neighbors and John C. "Rip" Ford in 1848 and 1849—and to survey the Rio Grande to see if steamboat navigation were feasible. "The country in question is uninhabited, except the neighborhood of Presidio del Norte," Johnston concluded, producing a map that left blank the entire bend of the river—the portion from above present-day Lajitas to the vicinity of Langtry—except for a modest area between Santa Elena and Mariscal Canyons, where the Comanche Trail crossed the

Rio Grande.[22] Captain S. G. French of the Quartermaster's Department put it more bluntly: "When the nature of the country is seen by those who may hereafter pass over the road, it may excite surprise; but it will not be that so practicable a route has been found, but rather than any was found at all."[23] The one lasting result of these early military efforts was the name "big bend," which Lieutenant William H. C. Whiting applied in his 1849 report, but which was only a dotted line on Johnston's map.[24]

The engineers began a more sustained effort in 1852 as a part of the international boundary survey. The Treaty of Guadalupe Hidalgo, which ended the war between the United States and Mexico in 1848, specified that the two countries jointly survey the new boundary. They began by establishing initial points at San Diego and El Paso del Norte, where the boundary intersected the Rio Grande, then set out to survey the entire border from Brownsville to the Pacific. They reached the Big Bend in August. In a meeting at Presidio del Norte with the newly appointed Mexican Commissioner José Salazar Ilarregui and Colonel Emilio Langberg, the Chihuahua military inspector, U.S. Chief Surveyor William H. Emory planned the survey of the most difficult section of the river, from Presidio to the mouth of the Pecos River—the heart of the Big Bend Country. Then he ordered his assistant, Marine Tyler Wickham Chandler—a magnetic and meteorological recorder, collector of specimens for the

Smithsonian Institution, and the son of a Whig congressman—into that jumble of desert, mountains, river, and canyons, "by far the largest portion" of which, Emory believed, "had never been traversed by civilized man."[25]

That was proved untrue when Colonel Langberg gave the Americans a copy of a rough map that he had made on a reconnaissance along the Mexican side of the border the previous year, and the thirty-three-year-old Chandler enthusiastically set out on September 12 with a team of surveyors and a military escort to add his modicum of geographic knowledge to the growing catalogue of data about the West that one day might reveal, in the words of Harvard University scientist Louis Agassiz, "the thoughts of the Creator."[26] Following an uneventful float through Bofecillos Canyon, with the military escort following along on the bank as best it could, the surveyors confronted the Great Cañon San Carlos, as they called Santa Elena Canyon. Chandler climbed up onto the Mesa de Anguila (Mesa of the Eels; a term perhaps corrupted from *angel* or *aguila,* eagle) on the Texas side and looked down at the river, some 1,500 feet below. "Dashing with a roaring sound over the rocks, the stream, when it reached the canyon, suddenly becomes noiseless, and is diminished to a sixth of its former width," he reported.[27]

Chandler was probably looking at the now-famous Rockslide, which makes Santa Elena a dangerous float in high water, even for an expe-

rienced boater. The Rockslide is made up of huge boulders, some perhaps fifty feet in height, according to Robert T. Hill, who negotiated the canyon in 1899, which completely block the river at low water and at high water form a dangerous rapids. In either case, Brewster County surveyor John T. Gano chose to portage around the obstacle during his 1882 mapping of the canyon. With the water a bit high, Chandler decided not even to risk the passage. Evidence of the wisdom of his decision came after they set a "strong wooden boat" adrift in the current at the entrance to the canyon and later found its "broken fragments" along the river below. Chandler estimated that the canyon was about ten miles long, with the river leaving—at the now-famous canyon mouth in what is today Big Bend National Park—"with the same abruptness that marks its entrance."

Below Santa Elena, they passed the *Vado de Fleche,* or Ford of the Arrows, and made their way into Mariscal Canyon, the surveyors in boats, the military escort trailing along and keeping watch from the peaks of the overlooking mountains. There are two major rapids in Mariscal: the Rockpile, a miniature version of the Santa Elena Rockslide, and the Tight Squeeze, where a large boulder blocks about two-thirds of the river channel. It was probably here that Chandler lost one of his boats, including the supplies that it carried. Switching to the Mexican side of the river, they paused at the ruins of San Vicente, an abandoned Spanish presidio, and left a survey flag and a note for the Mexican team. From there they would have marveled at the vista of the "half circle" of the Rio Grande as it begins its sweeping turn from southeast to northeast.

They intended to follow the river through what is today called Boquillas Canyon and on into the Lower Canyons, but found it impossible. "Rocks are here piled one above another, over which it was with the greatest labor that we would work our way," Chandler reported. His men existed on the barest of rations, and "the sharp rocks of the mountains had cut the shoes from their feet, and blood, in many instances, marked their progress through the day's work." They suspended the survey. "Beyond the Sierra Carmel," as Chandler called Boquillas, "the river seemed to pass through an almost interminable succession of mountains. Cañon succeeded cañon; the valleys, which alone had afforded some slight chances for rest and refreshment had become so narrow and devoid of vegetation that it was quite a task to find grass sufficient for the mules." With the assistance of a local Mexican guide, Chandler and his party completed their heroic tour by marching eastward, directly across the *despoblado,* to Fort Duncan at Eagle Pass.

Emory ordered Lieutenant Nathaniel Michler to complete the survey from Boquillas to Eagle Pass the following year. Michler found the point where Chandler had suspended the work but agreed, "It was next to an impossibility to approach the river for the first twenty miles of the survey." After riding and walking sometimes twenty or thirty miles around a mountain just to advance the survey a few hundred feet along the river, Michler decided that it would be easier to conduct the survey from the river, so he put his two skiffs and a flatboat in at Lipan Crossing. From there "the river forces its way through a deep canon nearly twenty miles in length, its banks being composed of high perpendicular masses of solid rock, resembling more the work of art than of nature," he wrote. At what might have been Burro Bluff (Upper Madison Falls) he ran into "a dangerous rapid . . . several hundred feet in length, extending from bank to bank." The skiffs made it through the "foaming and tumbling" current, waterlogged but still afloat. The flatboat proved to be "totally unmanageable." Crashing into the canyon walls, it began to sink. Only with difficulty did they pull it ashore and salvage the supplies onboard.[28] When Michler arrived at Eagle Pass, the engineers declared this portion of the survey complete, even though they had skipped the two largest of the canyons, Santa Elena and Boquillas.

With their scrutiny of this remote region, the engineers and scientists of the boundary survey added numerous exotic species of flora and fauna and crucial geographic knowledge to the growing natural history lexicon. But, perhaps most important, they had discovered another of those awesome pockets of the American West; the Big Bend Country was, Emory wrote, "one of the most remarkable features on the face of the globe."[29] The engineers interpreted the Big Bend landscape within the romantic tradition. Of the several landscapes that draftsman Arthur C.V. Schott produced, two, for example, the *Entrance to Cañon of San Carlos, Rio Bravo del Norte,* include small figures of Indians—nature's noble savages—in the foreground gazing longingly at the same majestic landscape that had transfixed the members of the survey team, alert to hear their "inner voices."

The language of the sublime—"exhilarating terror," in Hugh Honor's phrase—permeates their reports of the region's topographic features.[30] Emory wrote of the "stupendous rocky barriers" (p. 11), "chasms blocked up by huge rocks" (p. 11), "impending heights" (p. 11), and "inevitable destruction" (p. 11). During his heroic trek through the heart of the Big Bend, Chandler saw "sterile plains" (p. 81), "grand and imposing" passages (p. 82), and "dashing" rapids that made a "roaring sound" (p. 82). The hallmark of the country was its "rugged nature" (p. 82). Inside the "rocky dungeons" (p. 84), Chandler found unequaled "ruggedness and grandeur" (p. 83), concluding that, "No description can give an idea of the grandeur of the scenery through these mountains. There is no verdure to soften the bare and rugged view; no overhanging trees or green bushes to vary the scene from one of perfect desolation" (p. 84). Michler's route through the Lower Canyons was made up of "precipitous ascents and descents" (p. 74), "immense chasms" (p. 75), "steep" and "stupendous" (p. 77) cliffs that, until the last moment, concealed "fearful depths" (p. 75), and "tortuous" (p. 76) turns in the river. He noticed the "parched barrenness" (p. 75) of the Great Comanche Trail and navigated rapids, "foaming and tumbling in a furious manner" (p. 80), to finally overcome "insurmountable obstructions" (p. 78) to reach Eagle Pass. Even the geologist C. C. Parry wrote of "a lofty barrier," "deeply cut chasms," "precipitous walls" (p. 49), "bristling crags," "foaming rapids," a "dizzy height," "yawning abyss," "abrupt falls" (p. 53), "stupendous chasm" (p. 57), "arid and bleak sterility" (p. 59), and the "truly awful character of this chasm" (p. 55).

Despite the comprehensive nature of Emory's *Report,* its limited circulation and academic style meant that mystery and hyperbole rather than accurate information subsequently formed the public's image of the Big Bend as an impenetrable desert. Cattlemen had begun to arrive in the Big Bend as early as 1854 to supply beef to the troops at the newly established Fort Davis. Overland caravans, freight wagons like those operated by August Santleben of San Antonio, and mail carriers now rumbled across West Texas in increasing numbers and relative safety. Comanche resistance ended in 1874 with Comanche Chief Quanah Parker's defeat near Adobe Walls, and Colonel Ranald S. McKenzie's surprise of a large camp of Comanches and Cheyennes in Palo Duro Canyon. A tribe of Mescalero Apaches under Chief Victorio held out until 1880, when Colonel Benjamin H.

Grierson forced them into northern Chihuahua, where Mexican troopers killed the chief. Still, the Big Bend's reputation for bandit raids and mysterious characters persisted.

Commercial mining of silver in nearby Shafter in Presidio County in 1882 and in Boquillas a few years later and the completion of the railroad between San Antonio and El Paso in 1883 aroused further interest. That same year, the editor of the *El Paso Daily Herald* appealed to other newspapers in the state to contribute to an expedition to confirm rumors of the "sublime and majestic scenery" in the Big Bend. "Texas is about to eclipse anything that has heretofore been produced within the limits of North America," he predicted. But his plea fell on deaf—or at least impecunious—ears. It was not until 1899 that Robert T. Hill—a printer, journalist, cowboy, Cornell University–trained geologist, and former assistant professor at the University of Texas—undertook the expedition into "Darkest Texas" on behalf of the U.S. Geological Survey. Even then, the Big Bend's reputation as the "Bloody Bend" frightened Hill's men so much that two of them deserted before the expedition had even begun.

That reputation began to change in 1916, when the seething revolution in Mexico boiled over into a raid on the small communities of Glen Springs and Boquillas. Thousands of troops rushed into the Big Bend. General Hugh Scott, the army chief of staff, ordered Troops A and B of the 8th Cavalry under Major George T. Lang-

horne to the region. President Woodrow Wilson called out thousands of national guardsmen, who served throughout the Big Bend—at Alpine, Marfa, Marathon, Stillwell's Crossing, La Noria, and many other places—and saw its sublime scenery firsthand. Among them was Jodie P. Harris of Company I, 4th Texas Infantry, from Mineral Wells. An amateur cartoonist, Harris drew and lettered a four-page newspaper called *The Big Bend,* "a Paper with a Muzzle without a Mission," which was engraved by the *Fort Worth Record* and printed in Marfa. He also caricatured the guardsmen on postcards that he mailed home, where they were displayed in the local drug store. Like most soldiers expecting a fight but instead serving guard duty, Harris reported the overwhelming dullness of military duty, relieved in this instance by the spectacular scenery. He was one of the first to suggest in his caricatures that the Big Bend be made into a national park.

Texas artists discovered the Big Bend shortly after the National Guard went home. Dallas artist Frank Reaugh might have been the first professional artist to visit the region after the draftsmen of the boundary survey. Reaugh was born in Illinois but had moved to Texas with his family at an early age. He studied at the St. Louis School of Fine Arts and the Académie Julian in Paris, returning to establish his studio and teach art in Dallas. Traveling first by buggy and then in La Cicada (a Model A bus that he acquired and outfitted for the occasion), he introduced an entire generation of fledgling art students to

West Texas and the Big Bend through his annual sketching trips. "Passed through many canons and mountains," he noted in his "Log Book" on July 21, 1921, near Fort Davis. "Made sketch of Star Mountain."[31] Other sketches are labeled "Chisos Mountains" and "Big Bend."

While American regionalist painters Grant Wood and John Stewart Curry searched the Midwest for America's essential character, Texas artists such as Jerry Bywaters, Otis Dozier, Alexandre Hogue, William Lester, and Everett Spruce, some of whom had made their first trip to West Texas with Reaugh, discovered the Big Bend.[32] Terrain that had reminded the ancient Indians of a pile of leftovers abandoned by an indifferent Creator and that later qualified as a testing ground for the NASA astronauts simulating the moonscape now held strong appeal to these young artists who were searching for the regional distinctions that give Texas its "special character of place."[33] The frequent juxtapositions of nature's extremes attracted them: desert lowlands and alpine heights, intense sun and shade, and, until the recent pollution of the atmosphere by the coal-burning electric plants at Piedras Negras, intense clarity of vision. The engineers of the boundary survey had first commented on lucidity of the air, noting that they always seemed to underestimate distances because they were unaccustomed to being able to see so far. The first trained landscape painters to reach the Great Plains had marveled at the vast, horizontal vistas and clear sky, and artist Frederic Reming-

ton had frequently spoken of the Southwestern light as a shaping element in his palette. Similarly, the Trans-Pecos sun pours virtually unfiltered rays on its helpless subjects, while, at the same time, creating opaque but intriguing shadows. It is not an accident that clear, bright light is a dominant theme for the truthful artist working in the Big Bend, or that its translucent atmosphere is one of the compelling elements of Dennis Blagg's impassioned images. The resulting abstractions of nature draw artists and photographers back year after year. Just as the wilderness had asserted its influence over nineteenth-century landscapists, so the Big Bend had captured the generation of the Great Depression.

The movement to set a portion of the Big Bend Country aside as a public park gained momentum after Everett E. Townsend, former sheriff of Brewster County, was elected to the state legislature in 1932. Townsend had first seen the Chisos Mountains in 1894, while an inspector for the U.S. Customs Service in Presidio. Following the trail of some suspected smugglers, he reached the peak of Bandera Mesa, on the Brewster–Presidio County line north of Lajitas, with a beautiful valley laying some 1,200 feet below him. He saw the Chisos, about forty miles in the distance. They might have hovered above low-lying clouds, seemingly floating in the distance. Perhaps that is how they got their name—Chisos, some say, the "ghost" mountains. Or, perhaps he had such a crystal-clear view of the craggy peaks that it might have seemed that he

could reach out and touch them. Whatever, it was a view that "would have stirred the sluggish soul of a Gila monster," he said. He was so deeply impressed that he noted this intensely spiritual moment in his "scout book."[34]

Townsend, no doubt, remembered that experience years later, in 1933, when Abilene legislator R. M. Wagstaff approached him to ask if it were true that the Big Bend contained all the distinctive scenery that he had just read about in Robert T. Hill's 1900 *Century Magazine* article on the Rio Grande. Townsend quickly produced some photographs to document the claims, and the two West Texas lawmakers successfully shepherded a bill for Texas Canyons State Park through the legislature and onto the desk of Governor Miriam A. "Ma" Ferguson, who signed it. Townsend introduced another bill in a special session later that year that added more than 150,000 acres to the park, and Wagstaff attached an amendment that changed the name to Big Bend. President Franklin D. Roosevelt authorized the establishment of a Civilian Conservation Corps camp in the Chisos Basin the following year.[35]

Townsend now turned his efforts toward getting a national park for Texas, which had none. In 1934 the chief investigator of proposed national park sites, Roger Toll, superintendent of Yellowstone National Park, visited the Big Bend in the company of Townsend and historian J. Evetts Haley, collector of research in the social sciences at the University of Texas and director of the Texas Historical Records Survey. Toll came away convinced that the region had the potential to be of "national interest." On June 20, 1935, President Roosevelt signed into law the act enabling the establishment of Big Bend National Park. The legislature appropriated $1.5 million to acquire the remainder of the land needed for the park in 1941, and the nation's twenty-seventh national park opened in July, 1944. One of the most interesting aspects of the proposed park—one that only recently is nearing a satisfactory conclusion—was the proposal to establish a similar preserve on the Mexican side of the river.[36]

The Big Bend Country came to public attention at a pivotal time in the state's history. Texas had long been dominated by agriculture, especially cotton farming, but the discovery of oil at Spindletop in 1901 and in the East Texas field in 1930 had changed things. By 1935 the total value of the cotton crop was approximately $161 million, while the value of crude oil produced in the state was more than $367 million. And those in charge of the upcoming Texas Centennial celebration in 1936 concluded that this was the perfect opportunity to celebrate this elemental change in selling Texas: first to Texans themselves, then to the nation.[37]

This involved a significant revision in what they considered to be the image of Texas. Until then, the dominant image of Texas might have been *Dallas Morning News* editorial cartoonist John Knott's caricature, "Old Man Texas," dressed usually in a broad-brimmed hat, string tie, and planter's vest and sporting a drooping white mustache.[38] Knott identified Old Man Texas with the majority of people in the state, who lived in rural areas and earned their living from farming when he first introduced the character in 1906, and, through reprints in national publications, Knott's caricature helped form the image of Texas for millions of Americans who had never visited the state. Old Man Texas drew his iconic strength from the South and cotton plantations. That was not the image of Texas that would be presented at the Centennial.

The Centennial theme featured the state's rich history with a healthy dollop of "ten-gallon hats, six shooters, high-heeled boots, Texas Rangers, bluebonnets, and sex," according to Ken Ragsdale.[39] They began to move the public's image of Texas from Southern agricultural to Western cowboying. Among the most popular and long-lasting images that came out of the Centennial are six handsome posters, produced by the Tracey-Locke-Dawson advertising agency in Dallas. Cowboys and/or cowgirls dominate four of the posters; another contains an image of the façade of San José Mission in San Antonio; and the sixth presents Texas as a "land of vacation contrasts," with images of the gulf coast and what appears to be the Monument Valley of Utah and Arizona, but is no doubt intended to represent the state's new national park, Big Bend, with two cowboys riding along the river in the foreground. Old Man Texas and his Southern farming cohorts were not to be a part of the modern Texas image.

If the Centennial poster was the Big Bend's debut as an emblem of Texas, today the region is an integral part of our visual vocabulary through the efforts of people like Carlyle Graham Raht, who wrote the first history of the region in 1919, *The Romance of the Davis Mountains and Big Bend Country;* the first park superintendent, Ross A. Maxwell, who began the process of turning overgrazed ranchland into a park and published one of the best-selling books about it, *The Big Bend of the Rio Grande: A Guide to the Rocks, Geologic History, and Settlers of the Area of Big Bend National Park* (1968); the ranch woman turned self-appointed Big Bend publicist and writer Hallie Stillwell, *I'll Gather my Geese* (1991); and the iconoclastic writer, photographer, and *curandero* W. D. Smithers, who lived in the Big Bend from the time that he arrived there as a teamster with "Black Jack" Pershing's troops in 1916 almost until his death in 1981, seemingly photographing every inch of it, *Chronicles of the Big Bend: A Photographic Memoir of Life on the Border* (1999).

Literally millions of tourists and countless artists have come and gone since then: painters like Frank Reaugh, Jerry Bywaters, Otis Dozier, Alexandre Hogue, and more recently the internationally known sculptor Donald Judd; photographers like Ansel Adams, Laura Gilpin, Jim Bones, and Peter Koch, who spent a career documenting the Big Bend. But one who especially identifies with this austere and emotionally charged landscape is Fort Worth artist Dennis Blagg, who adopted it as his own a decade and one-half ago and has documented it ever since in his huge landscapes.

You can almost walk into Blagg's massive landscapes, some measuring ten or eleven feet in width by almost four feet in height. In one desert portrait we are face to face with the hypnotizing back-and-forth of the sinewy ocotillo; in another, the willowy Rio Grande, so tainted with the wastes of the desert and upstream cities that you can almost feel the grainy texture in your hands but golden and ethereal under the last light of day; and in yet another, the cracked and fissured veneer of a particularly beguiling cliff. Here Blagg paints so vividly that we can almost see the razor-like rock shards that, after countless heatings and coolings by the relentless sun and desert nights, literally blast out of their niches.

The elaboration in his pictures is such that we identify with the familiar—the grasses and cacti, rocks, and arresting mountain backdrops that meld into the clear Big Bend sky—rather than grasp the fact that this harsh and inhospitable landscape is a desert of biblical proportions, fit for an Elijah. In other paintings, the candidly portrayed desert floor is an essential contrast to a rhapsodic sky, while the distant mountains mediate between the two. Here unchanged nature—seemingly barren mountains with lechugilla, creosote, and sagebrush in the foreground—sets

off a turbulent sky, and the play of the bright sun upon the stunning cloud formations of the desert bestirs an uncommon reverence. Blagg has painted a "spellbinding," "mysterious," "haunting" desert that, in the case of a particularly exotic "pile of rocks," "seduced" him.

But words like "desolate" and "stark" crop up in his vocabulary, suggesting that he knows the other side of the desert, too. The image of dry and spindly ocotillos "pleading desperately" with the fast-moving clouds for water illustrate the "unforgiving and hostile" desert that holds the power of "life and death" over its flora and fauna, and humans, too, should they cast themselves upon its mercy. On occasion the billowy clouds that usually burn off in the heat of the day coalesce into Noachian thunderstorms that produce raging torrents, chasing the horned frog and the roadrunner from parched gullies and draws. Even in the midst of drought, evidence of flash floods may be seen in the grasses and trees swept down the draw. In another picture, Blagg's menacing and looming sky becomes the backdrop that sets off a drenched earth, alive and vivid with color after the refreshing shower and infused with the energy of the passing thunderstorm, whose negative ions replenish, for the moment, the earth's ozone supply.

That Blagg's realistic—indeed, almost photographic—panoramas foster such personal moments is reminiscent of the attitudes of the Comanches and Apaches and scientists and engineers almost 150 years ago—and of J. Frank

Dobie's civilized person. These portraits, like many of the pictures by the survey draftsmen, show an "uninhabited" land, in that they contain no images of human kind, and few of them show any evidence of people at all—perhaps an occasional highway to call to mind human passages, the goings and comings, both literal and figurative, across the landscape. And for similar reasons. Both purposely left people out because they want us to focus on the land itself—this rugged, pristine, seemingly ageless, and fragile desert—from which they—*we*—draw spiritual energy.

NOTES

1. Quoted in Dan Flores, *Horizontal Yellow: Nature and History in the Near Southwest* (Albuquerque: University of New Mexico Press, 1999), p. 1.

2. Dennis Blagg, interview with Ron Tyler.

3. For the history of the Big Bend, see Ron Tyler, *The Big Bend: A History of the Last Texas Frontier* (College Station: Texas A&M University Press, 1996).

4. Tyler, *Big Bend,* p. 66.

5. Paul H. Carlson, *The Plains Indians* (College Station: Texas A&M University Press, 1998), p. 85.

6. See Daniel J. Gelo, "'Comanche Land and Ever Has Been': A Native Geography of the Nineteenth-Century Comanchería," *Southwestern Historical Quarterly* 103 (Jan., 2000), 273–307.

7. Franklin W. Daugherty and Luis López Elizondo, "New Light on Chisos Apache Indian Chief Alsate," *The Journal of Big Bend Studies* 8 (1996): 33–49; Ron Tyler, et al., *New Handbook of Texas* (6 vols.; Austin: Texas State Historical Association, 1996), vol. 2, p. 90; vol. 3, p. 1154; Virginia Madison and Hallie Stillwell, *How Come It's Called That? Place Names in the Big Bend Country*

(Albuquerque: University of New Mexico Press, 1958), pp. 26–27.

8. Madison and Stillwell, *How Come It's Called That,* p. 68.

9. Tyler et al., *New Handbook of Texas,* vol. 2, p. 245.

10. See maps by or after Juan Pedro Walker in Jack Jackson, *Shooting the Sun: Cartographic Results of Military Activities in Texas, 1689–1829* (2 vols.; Lubbock: The Book Club of Texas, [1999]), vol. 2, pp. 327, 400.

11. Mabelle Eppard Martin, "California Emigrant Roads through Texas," *Southwestern Historical Quarterly* 28 (Apr., 1925): 287–301; Ernest Wallace and E. Adamson Hoebel, *The Comanches: Lords of the South Plains* (Norman: University of Oklahoma Press, 1952), p. 299.

12. Mabelle Eppard Martin, ed., "From Texas to California in 1849: Diary of C. C. Cox," *Southwestern Historical Quarterly* 29 (July, 1925): 47.

13. Hugh Honor, *Romanticism* (New York: Harper & Row, Publishers, 1979), pp. 16, 18.

14. Roderick Nash, *Wilderness and the American Mind* (rev. ed.; New Haven: Yale University Press, 1973).

15. Ibid., p. 78.

16. Ibid., pp. 80–81; quoted from Cole, "Essay on American Scenery," *American Monthly Magazine* 1 (1836): 4–5.

17. Quoted in Nash, *Wilderness and the American Mind,* p. 85.

18. Webber writing under the pseudonym of Charles Winterfield, "American Ornithology," *American Review: A Whig Journal* 2 (Mar., 1845): 274.

19. John I. H. Baur, ed., *The Autobiography of Worthington Whittredge, 1820–1910* (New York: Arno Press, 1969), p. 48.

20. George Hughes, *Fragrant Memories of the Tuesday Meeting* (New York: Palmer and Hughes, 1886), pp. 57–58. I am indebted to Kelly Mendiola for bringing this note to my attention.

21. Quoted in Tyler, *Big Bend,* pp. 75–76.

22. Quoted in ibid., p. 80.

23. William H. Goetzmann, *Army Exploration in the American West* (Austin: Texas State Historical Association, 1991), p. 231.

24. Lieutenant Whiting made reference to the Big Bend in his journal on March 12, 1849. See "Journal of William Henry Chase Whiting, 1849," in Ralph P. Bieber, ed., *Exploring Southwestern Trails, 1846–1854: Philip St. George Cooke, William Henry Chase Whiting, Francois Xavier Aubry* (Glendale, Calif.: Arthur H. Clark Company, 1938), p. 265.

25. Emory to Chandler, Presidio del Norte, Aug. 8, 1852, in William H. Emory Papers (Western Americana Collection, Beinecke Rare Book and Manuscript Library, Yale University, New Haven, Conn.); Emory, "Personal Account," p. 11. See also Tyler, *Big Bend,* p. 82.

26. William H. Goetzmann, *Exploration and Empire: The Explorer and the Scientist in the Winning of the American West* (Austin: Texas State Historical Association, 2000), p. 304, quoting Louis Agassiz, *Methods of Study in Natural History* (17th ed.; Boston: Houghton Mifflin, Co., 1886), p. 64. Further proof of previous explorations in the Big Bend is offered by Juan Pedro Walker's 1805 "Mapa Geografico" (Center for American History, University of Texas at Austin), with the Bolsón de Mapimí in the center. See the map reproduced in Jackson, *Shooting the Sun,* vol. 2, p. 327.

27. Material on Chandler's survey comes from his report, "San Vicente," in *Report on the United States and Mexican Boundary Survey,* vol. 1. The quotation comes from page 28.

28. Michler report, in William H. Emory, *Report on the United States and Mexican Boundary Survey* (2 vols.; 34th Cong., 1st Sess., H.E.D. 135), vol. 1, part 1, pp. 76, 79–80.

29. Emory, "General Description of the Country," in *Report on the United States and Mexican Boundary Survey,* vol. 1, p. 42.

30. Honor, *Romanticism,* p. 57. Page references that follow are to Emory, *Report on the United States and Mexican Boundary Survey,* vol. 1.

31. See Reaugh's Log Book for July and August, 1921, in the Frank Reaugh Papers, Box 2H451, Center for American History, University of Texas at Austin. See also Donald L. Weismann, *Frank Reaugh, Painter to the Longhorns* (College Station: Texas A&M University Press, 1985).

32. Lea Rosson DeLong, *Nature's Forms / Nature's Forces: The Art of Alexandre Hogue* (Norman: Philbrook/University of Oklahoma Press, 1984), pp. 9–10.

33. Rick Stewart, *Lone Star Regionalism: The Dallas Nine and Their Circle, 1928–1945* (Austin: Texas Monthly Press, 1985), p. 59.

34. Lewis H. Saxton and Clifford B. Casey, *The Life of Everett Ewing Townsend* (Alpine: West Texas Historical and Scientific Society, 1958), publication no. 17, p. 40.

35. John Jameson, *The Story of Big Bend National Park* (Austin: University of Texas Press, 1996), pp. 24–25, 27.

36. Ibid., pp. 30, 43–44, 120.

37. For background on the Texas Centennial, see Kenneth B. Ragsdale, *The Year America Discovered Texas: Centennial '36* (College Station: Texas A&M University Press, 1987).

38. Maury Forman and Robert A. Calvert, *Cartooning Texas: One Hundred Years of Cartoon Art in the Lone Star State* (College Station: Texas A&M University Press, 1993), p. 56, with examples of "Old Man Texas" on pp. 61, 65, 67, 80, and 88.

39. Ragsdale, *The Year America Discovered Texas,* p. 142.

PAINTINGS

No. 1
Cloud Sweep
1994
Oil on Canvas
36" × 46"
A Private Collection

Passing through Weatherford, Vernon and I are
on our way to the Big Bend. The landscape goes
by as the clouds sweep us on our way. I love
starting a trip to the desert. It is a great escape
from all the snags and problems of everyday life
. . . just freedom and a sense that nothing will
stop us now.

No. 2
Desert Gold
1995
Oil on Paper
10" × 33"
Collection of Stuart and Scott Gentling

Driving all day is a religious experience. There is
something very Zen about looking out the window to see a site like this: pure desert gold.

No. 3
Shadowline
1995
Oil on Canvas
17" × 60"
Collection of William Tex Gross

It's August and the clouds are building over the Chisos Mountains. This painting depicts the rising heat from the desert floor with Crown Mountain off in the distance. The foreground is in shadow and is covered with the flora and fauna of what I would call a desert oasis. I love the mix of contrasting light—the coolness of shadow and the hot baking sunlight of a summer day.

No. 4
Black Clouds
1995
Oil on Canvas
48" × 72"
United States Automobile Association, Houston

Along the Chinati range two thunderheads are
building toward a moment of high drama. . . like
two titans clashing in the sky. Thunderheads can
build suddenly, providing an endless array of
dramatic shapes.

No. 5
Two Peaks
1994
Oil on Canvas
22" × 60"
Collection of Dr. Fred Aguilar

Approaching the entrance to the Basin we pass these two peaks along the Chisos Mountain range. The peak on the right is one of my favorites, Pummel Peak. The duality of this painting has something to do with the mystery of being a twin.

No. 6
Nugent Mountain
1993
Oil on Canvas
30" × 40⅜"
Museum of Fine Art, Houston

Another great formation is Nugent Mountain,
located on the eastern side of the Chisos Mountains. The painting is something I had to paint
twice before getting it right. The first attempt
was much larger. Something was lacking, just
didn't feel right. I gave it another go, and it made
all the difference. At last the sky and mountain
were in sync with each other. *Nugent Mountain*
has a graceful tilt. The sky reflects a musical quality. It is full of dramatic movement that gives the
painting a quiet tension.

No. 7
Dry Ocotillos
1989
Oil on Canvas
60" × 90"
San Antonio Museum of Art
Acquired with John and Karen McFarlin
Purchase Funds

Dry Ocotillos is a stark and desolate painting, not
an image that puts you at ease. There is a feeling
of desperation; the two ocotillos in the foreground seem to be pleading for a drink of water.
August has arrived, and rain is long overdue. I
am trying to express the life-and-death quality
of the Chihuahuan Desert. It can be unforgiving
and hostile.

No. 8
Mushroomer
1995
Oil on Paper
22¼" × 27¼"
A Private Collection

A giant mushroom cloud—much like that of an
exploding atomic bomb—rises over the distant
Chisos Mountains. The rising cloud seems big,
yet it is far from where we are standing. . . still
we can smell the faint odor of rain in the air.

No. 9
Boquillas Burnoff
1992
Oil on Canvas
26" × 40"
Collection of Ron Tyler

The morning sun is coming up. You can feel and
see the evaporation of moisture burnoff from the
Sierra Del Carmen near Boquillas, Mexico.

No. 10
Moonwalk
1998
Oil on Canvas
18" × 48"
Courtesy Meredith Long Gallery, Houston

Vernon Fisher has two sons who have at times joined us on our journey to the Big Bend. Vernon's youngest son, Moses, was a very energetic boy who often reached a site well ahead of us. He would usually double back to carry my pack, knowing I was weary from the hike. I painted this and had Moses painted in at one point, only to remove his figure and replace it with the moon. This seemed more appropriate, because I could never see Moses once he passed me. He would simply be gone.

No. 11
Boquillas Light
2000
Oil on Canvas
26" × 40"
Collection of Alan Friedman

I love this time of the day. The sun is long to the
west, casting shadows in some spots and lighting
up other parts of the landscape as though they
were on fire. Boquillas lays to the left side out of
sight. You can just see a glimpse of the river
through the gap.

No. 12
Boquillas Turn
1995
Oil on Canvas
41" × 126"
Collection of the Houstonian Club, Houston

This large painting is full of movement. Following the trail to Boquillas Canyon, I climbed to a point overlooking the Rio Grande. I was taken with the sweeping composition. The ocotillo stands alone in the foreground, acting as a conductor of a great orchestra.

No. 13
Running River
1997
Oil on Canvas
18" × 38"
Collection of Sandy and Dr. Richard Mellina

The Rio Grande meanders into the distance.
The last hours of the day are passing, casting a
golden glow to the running river. It looks like
a yellow ribbon.

No. 14
Blue Creek Morning
1995
Oil on Canvas
18" × 24"
Collection of Jeff Fort

Carousel Peak looms over the Blue Creek
Ranch. I love the shape. It looks like a nipple
peeking over the surrounding cactus, creosote,
and underbrush, which seem to come alive with
movement. The desert awakens.

No. 15
Dry Wash
1995
Oil on Canvas
20" × 30"
Collection of Peggy and Bill Oehmig

Along the Blue Creek Trail is a dry wash that
winds its way toward the Chisos Mountains. A
feeling of anxiety runs through this painting.
The sky was overcast but hot. I felt that the bare
tree was trying to flee something ominous. The
painting symbolizes different meanings for me.
My thoughts were about a difficult passage in
my life. I felt like that tree, stripped bare.

No. 16
Edifice
1995
Oil on Canvas
36" × 96"
Collection of Dr. Harry Rosenthal

While walking the dry wash at Blue Creek Ranch I came across this rock formation that stopped me dead in my tracks. I had to paint it. For me, *Edifice* is like a family portrait. I see Dan, my twin brother, and myself as the two "head-like" rocks on the top left simply because we have always been very close. My mother and father are part of the foundation: the jutting-out part is my mother, and the broken-away part, my father. The various other rocks obviously represent other members of my family. When I began the painting, all of this was a mystery, revealing itself only as I painted.

No. 17
Blue Creek Nightfall
1998
Oil on Canvas
36" × 54"
Collection of A. J. Brass

The full moon rises over the Blue Creek Ranch.
This painting is magical, almost mystical. The
swaying shapes of sotol silhouetted against the
coming nightfall add a supernatural quality. *Blue
Creek Nightfall* is one of my favorite paintings.

No. 18
The Wet Hills
1995
Oil on Canvas
12" × 36"
Collection of Carmalinda Blagg
and Dan Swerdlow

Elephant Tusk appears faintly in the distant
storm. Sun spots light the wet hills of Glenn
Springs Canyon. The combination of the land–
scape and the dark sky gives one the feeling of
standing on the moon.

No. 19
Passing Storm
2000
Oil on Canvas
40" × 60"
Collection of Bob and Jan Scully

A passing storm moves across the desert floor.
Moments like this are the essence of Big Bend:
a great spiritual cleansing.

No. 20
Golden Window
2001
Oil on Canvas
30" × 45"
Courtesy Meredith Long Gallery, Houston

Late in the day I was driving along the road
heading to the Blue Creek Ranch when I noticed the Window all aglow and dark storm
clouds building. I love moments like this—a
contrast of dark sky and sunlit landscape. I had
avoided painting the Window, simply because it
seemed too clichéd, but all that changed after
seeing it like this.

No. 21
Early Sky
1993
Oil on Paper
14" × 22"
Collection of Pam Summers
and Raymond Rains

Daybreak. The early morning sky brings forth a
new day. The Window appears on the distant
horizon just over the scattered brush.

No. 22
Dragon's Back
1998
Oil on Canvas
40" × 120"
Collection of Texas Christian University

Directly across from the Blue Creek Ranch is
a place I call Dragon's Back. The hills in the
middle distance, with the two sharp points,
remind me of a great dragon caught sleeping.
There is something medieval about this painting.
The sotol in the foreground look like hunters
stalking their prey. The fallen sotol is like a spear
pointing out the direction of the hunted, while
the late light alludes to a magical feeling from
another time.

No. 23
Three Storms
2000
Oil on Canvas
36" × 48"
Collection of Joe Wilkinson

Located along the Ross Maxwell Drive is one of
the most popular spots, Sotal Vista. This painting
captures three downpours passing gracefully
along the lower floor of the great Chihuahuan
Desert. The yucca and sotol plants give this
painting a feeling of elegant harmony.

No. 24
Half Light
1993
Oil on Canvas
42" × 132"
Collection of Chris and Dr. Fred Thomas

Half Light was one of the first long-format paintings that I did on a large scale. I consider it one of those benchmark paintings that seem to happen every few years. That marvelous light just catches the top of Cerro Castellan, so monolithic. The duality of the ocotillos—again, a twin issue—enhances the painting. The light hitting the Sierra Ponce in Mexico or Mesa de Anguila in Texas in the distance seems almost sullen. *Half Light* is an unflinching portrait of the Chihuahuan Desert.

No. 25
Desert Tango
1994
Oil on Canvas
36" × 52"
Collection of Robert Brown

Desert Tango is a painting full of passion. I can see
dancers intertwined in the ocotillo's silhouette,
spinning around one another. The washed-out
trail is like the shape of a tornado, adding to the
movement of this painting. The ocotillo symbolizes the harshness of the Chihuahuan Desert.
When the climate is dry and hot the plants look
brittle and arthritic; then the rains come, and the
plants are in full bloom. They seem to dance
when the desert winds blow. Their gentle swaying is nearly trance-inducing.

No. 26
Off Road
1993
Oil on Canvas
26" × 40"
Collection of Dr. Harry Rosenthal

We stop at a remote parking spot to take in the
last of what has been a beautiful day. The off road
from the parking area disappears into the dark
landscape.

No. 27
Dry Land
1999
Oil on Canvas
32" × 120"
Courtesy Meredith Long Gallery, Houston

This painting is about the mounting tension of a coming storm. The sound of thunder echoes across the desert floor. The soft foothills of the Chisos Mountains are cast into a dark shadow as storm clouds hold the promise of rain for a dry landscape.

No. 28
Passover
1997
Oil on Canvas
42" × 120"
Collection of the Modern Art Museum
of Fort Worth

This portrait of Pummel Peak is one of a handful
of paintings that I consider my best artwork. The
peak is caught in a passing storm; the desert is
still wet with rain as the sun lights up the color
in the foreground. In contrast to this, the dark
sky casts a haunting shadow over Pummel Peak.
After fifteen years of watching this spot, the right
moment had finally come. I added the tall stalks
of yucca and lechugilla spears at the end. They
give the painting a graceful flow.

No. 29
Blue Clearing
2000
Oil on Canvas
20" × 37"
Collection of Michael Shannon

Blue Clearing is another painting of Pummel
Peak that has a darker feeling than *Passover.* This
painting seems more intimate, perhaps because it
is a much smaller painting. The streak of blue
gives the painting some color. Overall the sky is
soft. I was thinking about Vermeer's painting
View of Delft and the wonder of his handling of
clouds. I saw the painting a few years ago at a
National Gallery show of twenty-one Vermeers.
Seeing that painting helped me envision the Big
Bend in a more intimate way.

No. 30
Casa Grande Burnoff
1995
Oil on Paper
14" × 23"
Collection of Carol and Jack Benson

I do these small paper pieces as preliminary work
for larger paintings. Sometimes they turn out to
be better, because of their spontaneous energy.
This painting of Casa Grande covered by the
morning clouds is one of the good ones. I love
the quality of light and the unusual aspect of the
peak of Casa Grande being half-hidden.

No. 31
Cliff Dweller
1996
Oil on Linen
18" × 24"
Collection of Jane Rector

Life finds a way. As we climb the Lost Mine
Trail we encounter an odd tree that seems to be
growing out of a rock—or hanging on for dear
life.

No. 32
Floor Shadows
2001
Oil on Canvas
30" × 40"
Collection of Harris, Finley & Bogle,
P.C., Fort Worth

The South Rim Vista is one of my favorite places
in the park. I did a small study on paper while
working on the painting *Chisos Vista*. Over the
years I found myself thinking that I needed to
take the idea to canvas. It is funny how art works:
I never know when I'm going to expand on an
idea. Ten years later I was still fascinated by this
image. Painting it on canvas was the only thing I
could do to get it out of my mind.

No. 33
Chisos Vista
1985–86
Oil on Canvas
72" × 144"
Rosewater Properties, Dallas

The hike to the East Rim is long and tiring, but the reward is this breathtaking view. From this vantage point I can see the cloud shadows moving slowly across the face of the desert floor. All I hear is the haunting sound of the whispering wind. It's one of those moments that makes my journey to this spiritual landscape so fulfilling.

No. 34
Vernon's Walk
1997
Oil on Canvas
26" × 40"
Collection of Richard Ellis

Vernon Fisher and I have known each other for
more than twenty years. He is one of those few
people I really trust and admire. The fact that
both of us are artists only makes the bond of
friendship stronger. We have very different per-
sonalities: he is outgoing and engages people
easily; I, on the other hand, am somewhat re-
served. I have learned a lot from him. Vernon is
the essential pragmatist. He sees the true nature
in things that we all encounter in our daily lives
and makes great art from it. A stop at the Dairy
Queen is not complete without his sharp wit
picking up on something unusual or funny that
nobody else would see. As always when I look
up the trail my old friend is well ahead of me.
That seems to be how it always is—he gets
there first.

No. 35
East Rim Passage
1985–86
Oil on Canvas
80" × 118"
Permanent Collection of the Museum of South
Texas, Corpus Christi

One subject that many artists have addressed in
their work is the subject of death. *East Rim Passage* was painted during the time of the loss of a
loved one. The painting was like a sanctuary
where I could go to escape the somber reality.
Painting *East Rim Passage* also led me to a better
understanding of what was happening, helping
me cope with the idea of death. In the painting
the tree is a symbol of the death itself. The tangle
of tree limbs represents the uncertainties and
confusion we encounter when a loved one dies.
Finally, the shadow creeping in the foreground
becomes the hand of death reaching out toward
the tree. The clear blue sky makes the sun-lit tree
seem cleansed, reminding me that this rite of
passage is natural and acceptable. Death is life's
final mystery. *East Rim Passage* metaphorically
reflects my innermost emotions about death.

No. 36
Morning Floor
1993
Oil on Canvas
25" × 45"
A Private Collection

Another morning in the Big Bend passes.
The sky is breaking up as I look toward the
McKinney Hills. I am thinking about the solemn
nature of this landscape. There is something fleeting about the moment. Morning in the desert is
a time of transition that gives way to another
beginning. Like life itself, the desert is always
changing.

No. 37
Chihuahuan Heat
1991
Oil on Canvas
80" × 120"
Permanent Collection of the Museum of South
Texas, Corpus Christi

The Chihuahuan Desert can become unbearably
hot in the middle part of the day. In fact, it can
be quite taxing physically to both the body and
the mind. I painted this image just before one of
the trips we take each year, knowing that I
wasn't in shape for the journey. The symbolism
in the painting expresses my uncertain feeling
about being ready to make the many difficult
hikes that lay ahead. The composition and place-
ment of the rocks represent the impediments to
be overcome as much as they also indicate sheer
physical barriers of the harsh landscape of the
Big Bend. *Chihuahuan Heat* is also a collage of
sorts. I composed the painting by piecing together several different photographs from one
site to create a new reality. The ocotillo in the
foreground beckons me forward, calling me to
the distant mountains, the hike I've feared. Even
the scattered clouds sloping upward indicate the
long climb ahead of me.

No. 38
The Lowlands
1995
Oil on Canvas
18" × 90"
Collection of Jacqueline Hamilton

Heading out of the Basin toward Santa Elena
Canyon, we pass the Christmas Mountains,
which lie northwest of the park. Each time we
make this run for some reason I notice the small,
volcanic "plug." Seeing it this time makes me
want to paint it with that intense light cast across
its face. The creosote brush in the foreground
seems to be on fire with sunlight. That slight
haze of dust in the distant left part of the painting gives it a hot, stale look. However, as your
eye scans across the horizon it is cooled by the
Christmas Mountains.

No. 39
Western Chisos
2000
Oil on Canvas
17" × 67"
Collection of Jack Blanton, Jr.

Late in the day as I was driving along the Ross
Maxwell Scenic Drive I stopped to take in the
setting sun. As I looked over my shoulder I
caught a glimpse of the sun-washed Chisos
Mountains. I am continually fascinated with
contrasting parts of the landscape, where light
and dark areas meet. They create an unusual
mood in a painting.

No. 40
Desert Icon
1987–94
Oil on Canvas
48" × 84"
A Private Collection

Sometimes an unusual experience will inspire
me to paint. We took the Chimneys Trail and
camped near this pile of rocks. All of a sudden a
big sandstorm blew in, and we broke camp to
move our tent next to the rocks. This rock formation was the only spot near enough to offer us
shelter from the biting wind of sand. We dug in
our camp site next to it and rode out the storm.
The next day as we were leaving I saw this pile
of rocks a little differently than before. The chimney had the presence of an old friend, and I
knew that I wanted to paint it. I find it interesting how the experience of enduring the storm
motivated this painting. I don't think I would
have painted the chimney otherwise. Before the
storm it had been just a pile of rocks. Afterward,
it was something else to me, a desert icon.

No. 41
Hoo Doo Rock
2000
Oil on Canvas
24" × 36"
Collection of Joe Wilkinson

There is a place called Tapado Canyon west of the Big Bend National Park. The canyon is full of strange rocks of unusual shapes and sizes. The place reminds me of the old *Lone Ranger* television show sets. Keep your eyes open for the canyon, or you will miss it as you drive along the river road.

No. 42
Tapado Canyon
1996
Oil on Media Board
12" × 38"
A Private Collection

This is the overview of Tapado Canyon as the sun sets in the west. Although, geographically, the canyon is not located within the Big Bend Park borders, I consider it a must stop. A strange, eerie presence in the unusual rock formations makes Tapado Canyon a special place.

No. 43
Fresno One
1992
Oil on Canvas
54" × 96"
The J. C. Penney Co., Dallas

Fresno One is another painting inspired by a difficult experience. We were camping out at this site. The weather seemed perfect. A light breeze had us thinking that it would be a pleasant night on the desert floor. Around midnight everything just stopped—no breeze, just the desert floor radiating an unbelievable heat. In a panic, we broke camp and headed for the Basin where temperatures would be ten to twenty degrees cooler. Unfortunately, we got lost and had to spend the rest of the night on a sand flat in the middle of nowhere. The night was long and hot. We stayed up talking till dawn, finally finding our way out to the Basin. *Fresno One* is a painting of the original campsite under the salvation of a breaking morning sky.

No. 44
The Tree Line
1995
Oil on Canvas
24" × 36"
Collection of Pam Summers
and Raymond Rains

You can tell if there is water in the desert by
looking for the álamos or cottonwood trees. This
particular site lies north of the park and is
known as the Santiago Draw. The Chisos Mountains are visible through the distant haze.

No. 45
Sacred Site
1995
Oil on Paper
22½" × 27¾"
Collection of Elizabeth and Harold Lawrence

There is an old graveyard near Terlingua just
outside of the Big Bend National Park. Restora-
tion is now underway to preserve this sacred site.
Many of the graves are more than a hundred
years old, and time has taken its toll on them.
Several headstones were placed during the year
1919—the date of a worldwide flu epidemic.

No. 46
Desert Turn
1989
Oil on Canvas
72" × 96"
A Private Collection

A passing storm leaves puddles of precious water
along the blacktop road. As the clouds break, a
clearing in the distance reveals the blue sky. I
painted this at a time of great self-doubt, adrift in
life's ups and downs. I suppose that this road
painting also reflects my personal journey as a
painter.

No. 47
Late Drive
1997
Oil on Canvas
36" × 96"
Collection of Belo, Dallas

Nothing is more beautiful than a late drive in the desert. Normally my work lacks any sign of human existence, so the car lights are a departure for me. This painting, however, really seemed to need something to give the landscape a sense of scale. Whenever I see a car out there I am reminded of how small we are compared to the magnificent landscape.

No. 48
Thunderhead
2001
Oil on Canvas
30" × 37"
Collection of Harris, Finley & Bogel,
P. C., Fort Worth, Texas

Heading to Santa Elena Canyon, we stop to
watch a huge thunderhead expand over the
Chisos Mountains . . . a breathtaking sight. The
majestic power of this landscape seems to be
embodied in that cloud.

No. 49
Grande Reflections
2000
Oil on Canvas
40" × 60"
Collection of Lisa Dorn

The back door to the Big Bend takes you along the river road that meanders along the Rio Grande. This approach is one of my favorite drives to the park and certainly one of the most dramatic. Close to sunset is the best time to take this route. Looking west I am forever captured by the Rio Grande's silent reflections of clouds that drift overhead.

No. 50
Golden River
1997
Oil on Linen
16" × 20"
Collection of Albert Van Amberg

The Rio Grande snakes through the mountains bordering Texas and Mexico. The river reflects a golden light as the sun sets in the west. The desert fades into darkness. We head home. A fiery majesty, an allurement that keeps calling me back to the relentless landscape known as the Big Bend.

DRAWINGS

No. 51
Casa Grande Burnoff
1997
Pencil on Paper
12" × 38"
Collection of the Modern Art Museum
of Fort Worth

This drawing is among a series of pieces that I
did using pencil and graphite powder. The sheer,
horizontal shape and vertical point of view make
a great contradiction of sorts. This format el-
evates the drama to give the drawing a grand,
sweeping panorama of Casa Grande.

No. 52
Dead Horse Turn
1999
Pencil on Paper
5¾" × 23¼"
Collection of Dr. Harry Rosenthal

As Vernon and I take a back road turn we see the sleek shape of Dead Horse Mountain.

No. 53
Wall Face
1989–97
Pencil on Paper
9" × 14"
Collection of Deborah and Dr. Frank Lonergan

I get the feeling that I'm being watched while
I'm walking in the desert. I think it's those ocotillos. They're everywhere.

No. 54
Morning Ocotillos
1998
Pencil on Paper
12" × 18"
Collection of Mi Mi Kilgore

This drawing has an edgy, brittle quality to it. I love the shapes of the ocotillo silhouettes against the morning sky.

No. 56
Gothic Landscape
1995
Pencil on Paper
9" × 14"
Collection of James Blagg

Heading up to the Window, I came across this unusual landscape, with its gothic personality. The spears of yucca and sotol and the large rock in the foreground, which looks like the head of a dead dragon, give the impression of another place and time. It's the same feeling of the painting *Dragon's Back*.

No. 55
Lechugilla
1992–97
Pencil on Paper
9" × 14"
Collection of Jeff and Annette Coolidge

The lechugilla plant embodies those characteristics that define the Chihuahuan Desert: harsh, cutting, and resilient.

124

No. 57
Mushroom Rock
1996
Pencil on Paper
10" × 7"
A Private Collection

This drawing is another example of the unusual rock forms in Tapado Canyon. It looks like a big mushroom to me.

No. 58
Dead Trees
1997
Pencil on Paper
10" × 14"
Collection of Jeff and Annette Coolidge

We top out the South Rim hike and see these
two dead trees. They stand on the edge of the
overlook. Dry and barren, these two most likely
met their fate from lightning.

No. 59
Dancing Trees
1995–97
Pencil on Paper
9" × 18"
Collection of Kelly Thompson

Along the Chisos Mountain South Rim are oak,
pine, and juniper trees. They bring a unique
beauty to the higher elevations of the
Chihuahuan Desert. I noticed these trees on a
South Rim hike because they seemed to be
dancing.

No. 60
Regal Rock
1998
Pencil on Paper
6" × 14"
Collection of the Artist

I am intrigued by the large outcroppings of Big
Bend's huge rock formations. They seem to rise
up out of the ground.

No. 61
Up Flow
1998
Pencil on Paper
14" × 6½"
Collection of Betty and Stewart Alcorn

The Rio Grande flows through the Santa Elena Canyon. We escape to the cool shade of the canyon walls. There is a something poetic about sitting here listening to the quiet and graceful movement of the Rio Grande's flowing waters.

No. 62
Ocotillo Outpost
2000
Pencil on Paper
7" × 23½"
Collection of Courtney Schmoker and
Steve Powell

Like centurions at their post, these ocotillos
keep watch.

No. 63
Hermit's Hut
1997–98
Pencil on Paper
9" × 14"
Collection of Dr. Harry Rosenthal

As we reach Old Maverick Road, we turn south
onto a dirt road, which takes us to Luna's Jacal.
Gilberto Luna, a farmer, built this hut as a place
to escape from serving in the Civil War. He spent
the rest of his life in the Big Bend. He lived to
be 108 years old, married six times, and fathered
some fifty-eight children. The hut still stands, as
resilient as Luna himself.

No. 64
Dead Heat
1992–96
Pencil on Paper
11" × 24"
Collection of Deborah and Dr. Frank Lonergan

Done as a study for the painting *Fresno One,* this drawing has always been one of my best works in pencil. *Dead Heat* is a portrait of the utter stillness and unbearable heat of the Fresno One campsite.

No. 65
Distant Desert
1997
Pencil on Paper
12" × 38"
Collection of the Modern Art Museum
of Fort Worth

This drawing is a spin-off from another idea that
did not pan out (at least not yet). I like to look
at these ideas in different formats from time to
time just to see what happens. The long format
really changes the characteristics of a piece by
forcing tension horizontally.

No. 66
The Tinaja
1998
Pencil on Paper
8½" × 14"
Collection of Leslie and Scott Solomon

This is a line drawing of the big tinaja, better
known as the Ernst Tinaja, which holds water
year-round. The walk up offers limestone and
shale arranged like stacks of flat rocks—an
unusual place.

No. 67
The Foothills
1997
Pencil on Paper
6" × 24"
A Private Collection

I have always been taken with the slanting slopes
and soft peaks of the foothills.

No. 68
The Up Trail
1996–97
Pencil on Paper
8" × 14"
Collection of Rose and Bob Gregerson

This drawing depicts a trailhead near Rio Grande Village that leads to an overlook of the river. The Chisos Mountains stand in the distance. Logs line the trail on the up slopes to keep erosion in check as well as to offer sound footing for hikers.

No. 69
Chisos Mountains
1994
Pencil on Paper
9" × 24"
Collection of Erin and Keith Gregg

Entering the park we pass the Chisos Mountains.
This drawing was done as a study for the paint-
ing *Two Peaks.* I see it as a classic portrait of the
Chisos as seen from the northeast.

No. 70
Sotol Vista
1998
Pencil on Paper
7" × 24"
Collection of Wendy and Clay Hook

Late in the day at Sotol Vista the wind blows,
sounding like a desert song. It is another magical
moment that reminds me that time is fleeting.
We are all like dust in the wind. The desert is
everlasting. . . and eternal.

ABOUT THE ARTIST

DENNIS BLAGG lives and works in Fort Worth, Texas. Art Space III in Fort Worth and Meredith Long & Company in Houston represent his artwork. His career spans some thirty years of one-man shows and group exhibitions in Texas and beyond. His paintings and drawings are in many museum, corporate, and private collections.

Born: Oklahoma City, Oklahoma, 1951
Education: Self-taught

SOLO EXHIBITIONS

2001 *Dennis Blagg—New Paintings,* Meredith Long & Company, Houston

1998 *Dennis Blagg—Desert Drawings,* Art Space III, Fort Worth

1997 *Dennis Blagg—New Paintings,* Meredith Long & Company, Houston

1995 *Dennis Blagg—Recent Paintings,* Meredith Long & Company, Houston

1995 *The Lowlands—Dennis Blagg New Works,* Art Space III, Fort Worth

1993 *Half Light—Dennis Blagg Recent Paintings,* Barry Whistler Gallery, Dallas

1992 *Borderline: Paintings by Dennis Blagg,* Tyler Museum of Art, Tyler, Texas

1991 *Assured Space: Dennis Blagg,* Amarillo Art Center, Amarillo, Texas

1990 *Desert Landscapes—Dennis Blagg,* Barry Whistler Gallery, Dallas

1987 *Dennis Blagg—Paintings,* Barry Whistler Gallery, Dallas

GROUP EXHIBITIONS

2001 *As It Is—Dennis Blagg & Linda Blackburn,* Art On Site—Four Walls, Fort Worth

1999 *Dennis Blagg & Daniel Blagg: Landscapes,* Museum of South Texas, Corpus Christi

1998 *Virtual Reality,* Modern Art Museum of Fort Worth

1997 *New Horizons,* Meredith Long & Company, Houston

1995 *Texas Myths,* Houston Museum of Fine Art

1994 *New Horizons,* Meredith Long & Company, Houston

1992 *Introspect,* NRH Gallery, North Richland Hills, Texas

1991 *Profiles 1: The Land,* Arlington Museum of Art, Arlington, Texas

A Sense of Place, Acquisitions in Texas Art, San Antonio Museum of Art

1989 *Works on Paper,* Barry Whistler Gallery, Dallas

1988 *Land,* ACA Gallery, New York City

Landscapes, Haggar University Gallery, University of Dallas, Irving, Texas

1987 *Small Wonders,* Barry Whistler Gallery, Dallas

Eight Texas Realist Painters, Frito-Lay, Inc., Plano, Texas

Texas Realism, Texas Fine Arts Association, Atrium Gallery, Moody Hall, St. Edwards University, Austin

1986 *Works on Paper—Inside Texas,* Barry Whistler Gallery, Dallas

Texas Time Machine, Sesquicentennial Exhibition, Cullen Center, Houston

1985 *At the Edge of Town,* Nave Museum, Victoria, Texas

Portraits, Ann Havens Gallery, Rochester, New York

1984 *American Seen,* Adams-Middleton Gallery, Dallas

Daniel & Dennis Blagg, New Paintings, The Fort Worth Gallery, Fort Worth

1982 *Fun and Games,* The Waco Art Center, Waco, Texas

1980 *Opening Show,* Huzzo-Blamb Gallery, Fort Worth

A Texas Trilogy, Contemporary Gallery, Dallas

The Grove Street Group, KERA Gallery 13, Dallas

1977 *Paintings and Drawings,* Thistle Hill, Fort Worth

1975 *Daniel & Dennis Blagg,* Fine Arts Gallery, Fort Worth

1974 *Daniel & Dennis Blagg,* Carr Gallery, Fort Worth

MUSEUM COLLECTIONS

Modern Art Museum of Fort Worth
Museum of Fine Art, Houston
Museum of South Texas, Corpus Christi
San Antonio Museum of Art

PERMANENT COLLECTIONS

Mr. and Mrs. Claude Albritton, Dallas
Betty and Stewart Alcorn, Forth Worth, Texas
Baker, Mills, Glast, Dallas
Richard and Nona Barrett, Dallas
A. H. Belo Corporation, Dallas

Sonny Burt and Robert Butler, Dallas
Mr. and Mrs. Karl Butz III, Fort Worth
Dayton Art Institute, Rochester, New York
Mr. and Mrs. Edward Ducayet, Dallas
Harris, Finley & Bogle, P.C., Forth Worth, Texas
The Houstonian, Houston
Hughes & Luce, Houston
J. C. Penney Co., Plano, Texas
Locke, Purnell, Rain, Harrell, Dallas
Mr. and Mrs. John Marmaduke, Amarillo, Texas
Nations Bank, Charlotte, North Carolina
Nowlin Savings, Fort Worth
Pacific Enterprises, Dallas
Rosewood Properties, Dallas
Murray Smither, Dallas
Texas Christian University, Fort Worth
Texas Commerce Bank, Fort Worth, Dallas, and Houston
Texas Instruments, Dallas
Dr. and Mrs. Fred Thomas, Corpus Christi

BIBLIOGRAPHY

Akhtar, Susan. "Dennis Blagg Drawings." *Fort Worth Star-Telegram,* Arts, April, 1998.

Driscoll, John. *The Artist & The American Landscape.* Cobb, Calif.: First Glance Books, 1998.

Freudenheim, Susan. "Playing on Perspective." *Texas Homes,* March, 1986, pp. 19–21.

Greene, Alison de Lima. Texas: *150 Works from the Museum of Fine Arts, Houston.* New York: Harry N. Abrams, 2000.

Kutner, Janet. "Nature not Nurtured." *Dallas Morning News,* December 12, 1991, Section C, pp. 1, 4.

———. Preview, *Dallas Morning News,* Guide, November 29, 1991.

———. "Texas Artists Take a Turn Toward the Tangible." *Dallas Morning News,* Guide, July 5, 1996, p. 40.

New American Paintings 18 (fall, 1998): 14–15.

Nixon, Bruce. "Blagg's Landscapes Draw View Into Texas." *Dallas Times Herald,* May 8, 1987.

Review. Tyler Museum of Art, Tyler, Texas, September/November, 1992.

Tyson, Janet. "Grandscapes." *Fort Worth Star-Telegram,* November 1, 1993, Arts Section, pp. 1, 3.

———. "Landscapes Are Artists' Playground." *Fort Worth Star-Telegram,* November 30, 1991, Section G, pp. 1, 3.

———. "Seeing Landscapes in a Different Light." *Fort Worth Star-Telegram,* November 15, 1991, Arts Section.

Sime, Tom. "Land Futures." *Dallas Observer,* December 5, 1991, Artsweek, p. 31.

ISBN 1-58544-202-X

90000